MY FIRST PUPPET PICTURE BOOK
My
Favorite Animals

Pictures by Tadasu Izawa and Shigemi Hijikata

GROSSET & DUNLAP, NEW YORK

PUPPIES

Puppies are tiny and soft when they are born. Their little legs are weak— they can't walk. And their eyes are shut. Mother Dog must feed them many times a day.

At the pet shop there are many different kinds of puppies. They are all so cute and lovable that it is hard to choose just one. Each one seems to be saying "Please take me home with you—I will be your best friend."

Every time a puppy wags his tail,
he is telling you that he is happy
and glad to be with you. If you
have a puppy, remember that he is
only a baby. Pick him up carefully so
that you won't hurt or frighten him.

Puppies like clean things, just as
people do. If you are going to take
care of a puppy, you must remember
to keep his food and water dishes clean.
With good food and good care, he will
grow to be a fine, healthy dog.

Puppy's hair should be brushed
and combed often—just like yours.
When a puppy is about six months
old, maybe you can give him a bath.

As a puppy grows older, he may learn to understand different words you say, like "Sit!" or "Stay!" or "Lie down!" Of course, you must say these words many times and show him what to do.

A puppy can even learn to do funny
tricks, if you want him to. He can learn
to lie down and cover his eyes. Or he can
stand up on his back legs.

Most puppies like to play "Fetch-the-stick" or "Fetch-the-ball." When you have a stick or a ball in your hand, a puppy will wait for you to throw it. Then he will run to get it and bring it back to you in his mouth. He will want to play this game again and again.

The wonderful thing about a puppy is
that he will always love you. He will run
and play with you when you are happy.
And he will fall asleep beside you when
you are tired.

KITTENS

When kittens are born, their eyes are closed shut. Their little legs are so weak, they can only crawl around a bit. But they can find Mother Cat, and they snuggle close to her when they nurse.

Mother Cat picks a dark and quiet place for the family "nest," so that the kittens won't be disturbed by too much light or noise. Kittens can't take care of themselves at first. Mother Cat not only feeds them, but she cleans their furry faces and backs and tails with her tongue.

Sometimes Mother Cat may want to move to a different hideaway. She picks up each kitten in turn by a fold of skin at the back of the neck. She uses her mouth to pick up the kittens this way. It doesn't hurt the kittens. Somehow, Mother Cat knows this is the best way to carry the little ones.

About ten days after they are born,
kittens start to open their eyes. Then
they really have a chance to explore. But
they will not usually wander far from
where Mother Cat happens to be.

Kittens are very playful. A kitten will take a large button, or a wooden spool, or a ping-pong ball, and scoot it across the floor to another kitten, just as hockey players do with a puck on ice.

Outdoors, Mother Cat will teach
her kittens to lie still in the grass, to
hide, and to pretend to spring upon
something that moves. It is all a game at
first, but it is also a way of teaching the
kittens to hunt.

Oh, there's something fluttering by!
It's a butterfly! Kittens love to watch
anything that flies. One kitten jumps
high in the air, reaching out with its
paws. But it's like reaching for the
moon. The butterfly doesn't get caught.
It just keeps flying along, looking for
pretty flowers.

Sometimes
kittens wrestle.
They roll over and
turn somersaults
while they hold on
to each other.
They kick with
their back paws.
It may look as if
they are fighting.
But they are just
playing.

Of course, at the same time, they're learning to protect themselves. Mother Cat sometimes teaches these "lessons."

Kittens are frisky, adventurous, and curious. They get into all kinds of mischief. Sometimes a kitten will climb a tree, go out on a branch, and then be too frightened to get back down. Then someone has to rescue it.

Kittens are soft balls of fluff. And they love to take naps. Sometimes two kittens will lie next to each other, using each other for pillows. They feel warm and comfortable. Will you say good night to them in kitten language? "Mew! Mew!"

BUNNIES

You know what bunnies are, of course. That's right, they're rabbits. But because rabbits are so nice to have as pets, we have a pet name for them. We call them bunnies.

Bunnies don't walk or run. What do you suppose they do? Did you guess? Yes, bunnies hop! They have long, strong back legs that move them forward quickly.

HOP! The front legs are for balance. HOP, HOP, HOP! When one hop follows another, it almost looks as if they are playing "Leapfrog."

Pet bunnies live in special cages called
hutches, which people have made of
wood and wire. Pet stores have them.
Fresh hay is put on the bottom of the
hutch, and there is a place for the bunny
to get his food and water. Bunnies kept
in a hutch must be fed every day—and
the hutch must be kept clean, too.

A bunny's tail looks round, because it's covered with fluffy fur. It is about two inches long. And can you guess why a certain kind of bunny is called a cottontail? When the bunny hops along the ground, the white underpart of his tail turns up and looks like a bobbing ball of cotton!

What do bunnies like to eat? Most
bunnies eat clover, grass, lettuce,
cabbage, and leafy plants in the spring
and summer.

During the winter months, they may nibble the berries on bushes or gnaw on the bark of trees. Bunnies, like beavers, have special teeth for gnawing.

Most often, wild bunnies make their homes in marshes, swamps, and fields—places where they can hide in tall grass or weeds or bushes. Some bunnies live alone in a small hole that has been dug by another animal, such as a woodchuck or a skunk. When bunnies live together, they make a home under a pile of wood or twigs or underbrush.

Many bunnies have long ears. Their ears can catch sounds—even the faintest sounds—from any direction. Sometimes bunnies will move just one ear to do this. But they can also move both ears together.

Bunnies not only have good hearing. They also have a keen sense of smell. A bunny's nose can sniff out where a juicy carrot or other food may be. It can even tell where there may be danger. If you watch a bunny carefully, you will see that is twitches its nose every few moments. That makes a bunny funny!

Here is Monar the Magnificent
Magician, removing a bunny from a top
hat. Did you ever see a magician do that
amazing trick? Do you know why
magicians especially like bunnies?
Bunnies can't make a sound, and so they
won't tell how the trick is done!

FARM ANIMALS

The first light of the morning sun pushes the darkness away in the sky over the farm. "Cock-a-doodle-doo!" crows the rooster as he greets another day.

There are new eggs in the
henhouse. "Cluck, cluck, cluck!"
say the hens. "Cheep, cheep,
cheep!" say the baby chicks,
scratching about on the ground
for grain.

The cows walk from the barn to the pasture, where they like to munch the sweet, green grass. "Moo!" they say. Sometimes they rest in the shade of a tree, where it is cool. Cows give us delicious milk to drink.

Frisky lambs are playing together
down in the meadow. "Baa, baa!" they
say. When they grow up, they will be
sheep. Sheep give us wool for clothes
that keep us warm.

The little turkeys will grow big and fat.
They say, "Gobble, gobble!" as they move
through the grass, hunting for bugs
to eat.

At a nearby pond, baby ducks and geese are learning to swim. They seem to love the water. "Quack, quack!" say the big ducks. "Honk, honk!" say the big geese.

The hours pass. Soon it is noontime. The pigs and piglets, who have been sleeping in the sunshine, begin to wake up. "Grunt, grunt!" they say. It must be time for lunch.

The bunnies are nibbling lettuce and carrots for lunch. They don't make a sound, but they sometimes thump their hind feet on the ground. It's their way of talking to each other.

"Naa-a-a!" says Father Billy Goat. "Naa-a-a!" says Mother Nanny Goat. Goats give us milk, and cheese can be made from it. The goats like to jump and walk along the tops of large rocks and stony places.

"Neigh, neigh!" says the farmer's horse. He seems to be asking the children, "Would you like to go for a ride through the field of clover?"

Yes, the children surely would! Wouldn't you?